Easy Cakes & Bakes

CW00686721

Easy Cakes & Bakes

Margaret Clark

STELLAR BOOKS

Published in 2018 by:
Stellar Books
1 Birchdale
St Mary's Road
Bowdon
Cheshire
WA14 2PW

E: info@stellarbooks.co.uk
W: www.stellarbooks.co.uk
T: 0161 928 8273

ISBN: 9781910275214

Copyright ©Margaret Clark 2018

All images are copyright: Margaret Clark, Sean Bell and Bryan Bane ©2018

Printed by Williams Design and Print, Cheshire.

A copy of this book is available in the British Library.

The author has asserted her right under the Copyright, Designs and Patents Act 1988 to be identified as the author of this work.

All rights reserved. No part of this publication may be altered, reproduced, stored in a retrieval system or transmitted in any form or by any means, electronic, mechanical, photocopying, recording or otherwise, except as permitted by the UK Copyright, Designs and Patents Act 1988 without the prior express permission of the author.

To Mum, Dad and all my family
for all their support and encouragement

Acknowledgements

Many friends have helped in different ways to produce this book.

Firstly I would like to thank Roger my husband for his support, patience and help in getting this book up and running.

My daughter Suzanne and son Robert for all their support and computer knowledge.

My friend Karen Bolshaw for her support and for being at the end of the phone when I have needed her and for giving up her time.

Thanks must go to Williams Design and Print Byley for their time.

Many thanks too, to Sean and Bryan for the time they put into taking the photos.

Lastly but not least Patricia from Stellar Books. Without Patricia there would be no *Easy Cakes and Bakes* recipe book. She has helped me every step of the way.

Many thanks to all, and greatly appreciated.

Contents

Baking Over Time

My love of baking started from a very early age. Being a farmer's daughter and having a family who loved their food, there were always open mouths ready for a good slice of wholesome cake at bagging time. After leaving school I went to college and followed on with numerous baking and cake artistry courses.

In 1983 while I was on holiday with friends, my parents thought it was about time I started earning, so when I returned there was a job interview lined up for me in a Knutsford bakery. Starting early in the morning and working alongside an Irish foreman, making hundreds of sausage rolls, pies, bread and cakes, it was a bit of a shock to the system. I then moved on to making hundreds of eclairs, gateaux and birthday cakes which I much preferred.

In1987 the National Trust at Tatton Park decided it wanted fresh bakery as part of its fresh baker products, and they were looking for a baker to make their own bread rolls, cakes and tray bakes. This sounded like a challenge. Roger, my husband, made me a few baking trays, ovens and mixers were ordered, benches were delivered and away I started baking for Tatton Park. Within a short time the home baking seemed to take off so Roger had to make yet another ten trays and it was getting to a point where it needed two bakers in the bakery. We went from making two to three dozen cakes to three to four thousand cakes per week along with six thousand hand-made mince pies every year and 24 Christmas cakes… not to mention the bank holidays when we would make at least a thousand scones. When our daughter Suzanne arrived in1999, I had my kitchen registered and baked for Tatton from home as well as working there three days a week.

In 2001 the dreaded Foot and Mouth hit, and, as we had animals at home, I was isolated from working at Tatton, so I baked for the tea rooms from home for a couple of months. This then led to baking forty cakes a week for the housekeeper's store for them to sell in their shop which continued for a further three years after Tatton had reopened. In 2002 our son Robert arrived.

In time I increased my hours. In 2013 the Gardeners cottage opened at Tatton which required numerous afternoon teas along with more biscuits and more cakes. It was in February 2015 after meeting many people, receiving awards, meeting royalty and celebrities it was time for me to move on and let someone else take over my role as head baker.

One thing I have always wanted to achieve in life is to write my own recipe book, so after leaving Tatton it gave me this great opportunity to do something about it. I have chosen easy recipes which I am sure you shall have most if not all the ingredients in the cupboard.

Happy baking!

Margaret

Oven Temperatures

GAS	°F	°C	FAN
1	275°	140°	120°
2	300°	150°	130°
3	325°	170°	140°
4	350°	180°	160°
5	375°	190°	170°
6	400°	200°	180°
7	425°	220°	200°
8	450°	230°	210°
9	475°	240°	220°

Volume

IMPERIAL	METRIC
1 tbsp	15 ml
2 fl oz	55 ml
3 fl oz	75 ml
5 fl oz (¼pint)	150 ml
1 pint	570 ml
1 ¼ pint	725 ml
1 ½ pint	1 litre
2 pints	1.2 litres
4 pints	2.25 litres

Note: All ovens differ from one to the other so times and temperatures are only approximates.

Abbreviations

tsp	teaspoon
dsp	dessertspoon
tbsp	tablespoon
grd	ground
lb	pound

Weights

IMPERIAL	METRIC
¼ oz	10 g
½ oz	20 g
1 oz	25 g
1 ½ oz	40 g
2 oz	50 g
4 oz	100 g
8 oz	225 g
12 oz	350 g
1 lb	450 g

Useful Hints

Overcooked or cookies gone hard	Slice lemon in half and place in an airtight tin with the cookies overnight
Dropping egg shell in ready separated egg	Use a larger piece of eggshell to get it out with. It acts like a magnet.
Easy way for breaking walnuts	Place them in a plastic bag and crush with a rolling pin.
How to stop jam from boiling over in each jam tart	Drop 2 teaspoons of cold water in each one before baking.
How not to get crumbs on your knife when slicing cake.	Have a jug of hot water near and keep dipping your knife into it.

Egg Testing

Fresh Eggs

- Test in a glass of cold water. If the egg is fresh, it sinks.
- If the egg floats on top discard it.
- If the egg sinks to the bottom but stands on its point it still can be used but it's not quite as fresh.

Eggs for Baking

I use medium eggs for baking. A medium egg weighs between 50 - 60g, a large egg weighs approximately 70g.

Duck Eggs

Can be used for baking. They have a lovely bright yellow yolk which will give your cakes an attractive colour and they will rise more. Be careful with your weight as a duck egg weighs between 65 - 70g.

Milk

As a farmer's daughter I like to support the British farming community so I try and use milk in as many ways as possible.

Milk plays several roles in baking: it adds structure to batter and it adds protein. You will also get a lighter cake and it gives extra shelf life.

The difference between whole milk and semi-skimmed milk is the fat content: whole milk generally contains 3.5% fat while skimmed milk contains none. I personally prefer to use whole milk.

Milk is best used at room temperature for sponges and batters as the butter, eggs and sugar cream nicely with the added milk and you get a lighter end result. Also if you are short of eggs when making a cake you can always substitute with a little extra milk.

Loaves & Cakes

Apricot Loaf

8 oz/225g chopped dried apricots or prunes
10 fl oz/300ml water
4 oz/100g lard
6 oz/175g caster sugar
3 eggs
6 oz/175g self-raising flour
1 tsp ground cinnamon
6 oz/175g wholemeal flour

Method

1. Place apricots / prunes along with water, lard and sugar in a pan and bring to the boil.
2. When boiled, set aside to cool.
3. Meanwhile, grease and line a 2lb loaf tin.
4. Whisk the eggs together and sieve the flours and cinnamon.
5. When cooled add in eggs followed by flours and cinnamon mix until well combined.
6. Pour mixture into prepared loaf tin.
7. Bake for approximately 45 minutes.

This is a very moist cake and is lovely served in the afternoon with a cup of tea.

Banana and Walnut Loaf

Oven 170°C / 325°F / Gas 3

2 bananas
6 oz /175g margarine
4 oz /100g caster sugar
10 oz /275g plain flour
1 tsp baking powder
1 egg
2 oz /50g broken walnuts

Method

1. Mash bananas to a pulp.
2. Place margarine, sugar, flour, baking powder and egg into a bowl and beat until thoroughly combined.
3. Add walnuts and mashed bananas; beat again until soft consistency.
4. Pour mixture into a 2lb loaf tin.
5. Bake at 170°C 325°F gas 3 for approximately 45 minutes.

This loaf can be served with or without butter; it's very nice either way.

Bara-Brith

2 tea bags
1 mug boiling water
12 oz/350g mixed dried fruit
1 egg
4 oz/100g caster sugar
10 oz/275g self-raising flour

Method

1. Soak the fruit in the boiling water with the tea bags overnight.
2. Next day take out the tea bags, beat the egg and add along with the sugar until thoroughly combined.
3. Sieve the flour and fold into the mixture.
4. Pour mixture into a well-greased lined 2lb loaf tin.
5. Bake at 170°C 325°F gas 3 for approximately 1 hour.

This loaf is best kept in an airtight tin for a few days before serving.

Boiled Fruit Loaf

Oven 170°C / 325° F / Gas 3

10 oz/275g mixed dried fruit
5 fl oz/150ml water
4 oz/100g butter
4 oz/100g caster sugar
1 egg
8 oz/225g self-raising flour
4 oz/100g cherries

Method

1. Place fruit, water, butter and sugar in a pan and bring to boil.
2. When boiled set aside and leave to cool.
3. Line and grease a 2lb loaf tin.
4. Beat the egg and sieve the flour.
5. When mixture has cooled add in the beaten egg.
6. Fold in the flour and cherries.
7. Pour mixture into the prepared loaf tin and bake at 170°C 325°F gas 3 for approximately 1 hour.

This loaf is very tasty but will taste even better if kept in an airtight tin for a couple of days.

Carrot, Courgette and Ginger Cake

8 oz/225g margarine
6 oz/175g caster sugar
3 eggs
4 oz/100g grated carrot
4 oz/100g grated courgette

9 oz/250g self-raising flour
2 tsp baking powder
3 tsp grd ginger
2 tsp grd cinnamon
1 tbsp milk

Filling

2 x 8 oz/175g cream cheese
4 oz/100g butter

1lb/450g icing sugar
1 tsp lemon juice

Method

1. Cream margarine and sugar together. Beat the eggs in a separate bowl.
2. Sieve the flour, cinnamon, ginger and baking powder together.
3. Add the eggs and sieved flour alternately to the creamed mixture.
4. Stir in grated carrot and courgette.
5. Lastly add the milk and stir until a dropping consistency.
6. Pour mixture into a 9 inch greased, lined baking tin and bake for approximately 35 minutes.
7. Meanwhile make the filling: drain any liquid off the cream cheese. Mix the cheese and butter together.
8. Sieve the icing sugar and add along with the lemon juice to the mixture.
9. When cold, cut the cake in half and spread with a layer of cream cheese filling.
10. Spread cream cheese on top and decorate as desired.

Chocolate Beetroot Cake

8 oz/225g drained pureed beetroot
3 eggs
5 fl oz/150ml vegetable oil
3 fl oz/75ml milk
9 oz/250g caster sugar
8 oz/225g self-raising flour
1 tsp bicarbonate of soda
2 oz/50g cocoa powder

Filling
5 oz/150g plain chocolate
4 oz/100g icing sugar
3 fl oz/75ml double cream

Method

1. Combine beetroot, eggs, oil, milk and sugar together.
2. Sieve flour, bicarbonate of soda and cocoa powder together and add to the beetroot mixture.
3. Mix well until a soft consistency.
4. Pour mixture into a well-greased lined 9 inch cake tin. Bake for approximately 35 - 40 minutes.
5. Meanwhile make the filling: melt the chocolate in a bowl over a pan of hot water.
6. When the chocolate has melted, sieve the icing sugar into it and beat well.
7. Place the cream in a saucepan and bring to nearly boiling point.
8. Take off the heat and add in the melted chocolate.
9. When cooled, cut the cake in half and spread with the chocolate mix leaving some to coat the top with.

An unusual but very moist and moreish cake.

Cherry Loaf

4 oz /100g butter
4 oz /100g caster sugar
3 eggs
4 oz /100g cherries
4 oz /100g plain flour
4 oz /100g self-raising flour
2 tbsp milk

Method

1. Cream butter and sugar together.
2. Beat the eggs and add to the mixture.
3. Sieve both flours together and fold into the mixture along with 2oz/50g of the cherries.
4. Add the milk and mix well.
5. Place mixture into a greased and lined 2lb loaf tin.
6. Place remaining cherries on top and bake for approximately 35-40 minutes.

A very light refreshing loaf.

Chocolate Sponge Cake

Oven 170°C / 325°F / Gas 3

8 oz/225g margarine
8 oz/225g caster sugar
8 oz/225g self-raising flour
2 oz/50g cocoa powder
3 eggs

Buttercream Filling
5 oz/150g butter
10 oz/275g icing sugar
2 oz/50g cocoa powder

Method

1. Cream margarine and sugar together.
2. Sieve the flour and cocoa powder together.
3. Add in the eggs one at a time alternately with the sieved flour mix. Mix until a soft consistency.
4. Place mixture into a greased 8 inch round cake tin and bake for 35-40 minutes.
5. Remove from oven and leave to cool.
6. Meanwhile make the butter cream: sieve the icing sugar and cocoa powder together.
7. Cream the butter and icing sugar together.
8. When cooled, cut the sponge in half.
9. Spread the buttercream in the sponge and sandwich together. Dust with icing sugar if desired.

A traditional recipe which always goes down well.

Classic Swiss Roll

3 eggs
3 oz/75g caster sugar
4 oz/100g self-raising flour
8 oz/225g raspberry jam for the filling.

Method

1. Place the eggs and sugar into a mixing bowl. Whisk until thick and creamy.
2. Sieve the flour then fold into the egg mixture with a metal spoon.
3. Grease and line a 9"x12" Swiss roll tin.
4. Pour the mixture into the tray and bake at 170ºC 325°F gas 3 for 15 minutes until the sponge begins to shrink from the edges of the tin and is golden brown in colour.
5. Meanwhile lay a piece of greaseproof paper on the table and sprinkle with caster sugar.
6. Warm the raspberry jam for the filling.
7. When the Swiss roll is baked, turn out onto the greaseproof carefully pulling off the lined paper.
8. Spread the warmed jam over the Swiss roll and carefully roll, using the greaseproof to help you.
9. Leave to cool and serve.

A classic Swiss roll which also can be served with fresh cream if desired.

Coffee Sponge Cake

8 oz /225g margarine
8 oz /225g caster sugar
3 eggs
2 tbsp coffee granules dissolved in hot water
8 oz/225g self-raising flour

Method

1. Cream margarine and sugar together.
2. Whisk the eggs and dissolved coffee together.
3. Add the eggs alternately with the sieved flour.
4. Spoon mixture into a greased lined 8 inch round tin.
5. Bake 170°C 325°F gas 3 for 35-40 minutes till firm to touch.
6. Leave to cool.
7. Finish off with coffee butter cream (see page 154).

A very moreish cake.

Date and Walnut Loaf

8 oz/225g dates
½ tsp bicarbonate of soda
5 fl oz/150ml boiling water
2 oz/50g butter
4 oz/100g caster sugar
1 egg
8 oz/225g self-raising flour
1 oz walnuts

Method

1. Put the dates, bicarbonate of soda and water into a saucepan and cook until the dates form a pulp.
2. Leave date mixture to cool.
3. Beat together butter and sugar.
4. Add beaten egg then gradually add in flour, chopped walnuts and date mixture.
5. Mix thoroughly together.
6. Place mixture in a greased lined 2lb loaf tin.
7. Bake for approximately 1 hour.

A nice hearty ideal for when you are working on the farm.

Easy Lemon Yogurt Cake

Oven 170°C / 325°F / Gas 3

7 oz/200g caster sugar
Zest of 1 lemon
1 x 150g lemon yogurt
5 fl oz/150ml olive oil
10 oz/275g self-raising flour
3 eggs

Filling

Lemon curd

Method

1. Place all ingredients into a bowl and mix thoroughly.
2. Pour mixture into a greased lined 9 inch round cake tin.
3. Bake for approximately 170°C 325°F gas 3 for 35 - 40 minutes.
4. When cooled cut in half and spread with lemon curd.

Every Day Sponge Cake

Oven 170°C / 325°F / Gas 3

8 oz/225g margarine
8 oz/225g caster sugar
3 eggs
1 tsp vanilla extract
8 oz/225g self-raising flour

Buttercream filling
5 oz/150g soft butter
10 oz/275g icing sugar
3 tbsp raspberry jam

Method

1. Cream margarine and sugar together.
2. In a separate bowl, beat the eggs and vanilla together.
3. Add the eggs alternately with the flour to the butter and sugar mixture.
4. Mix until a soft consistency.
5. Place mixture into a greased 8 inch round tin and bake for 35 - 40 minutes.
6. Remove from oven and leave to cool.
7. Meanwhile make the butter cream: sieve the icing sugar.
8. Cream the butter and icing sugar together until light in colour.
9. Cut the sponge in half when cooled and spread with raspberry jam.
10. Spread the buttercream over the jam and sandwich the cake together, sieve icing sugar on top.

A very quick easy and delicious sponge

Madeira Loaf

Oven 170°C / 325°F / Gas 3

4 oz /100g butter
5 oz /150g caster sugar
2 eggs
6 oz /175g self-raising flour
1/4 tsp baking powder
1 lemon rind and juice
A little milk

Method

1. Cream butter and sugar together.
2. Sieve the flour and baking powder together.
3. Add the eggs, lemon juice and rind into the mixture followed by the sieved flour.
4. Mix well together adding a little milk to give a softer consistency.
5. Turn mixture into a greased lined 2lb loaf tin.
6. Bake at 170°C 325°F gas 3 for approximately 35 minutes until firm on top.

A lovely light textured loaf ideal with a cup of tea.

Parsnip Apple and Cinnamon Cake

9 oz/250g self-raising flour
2 tsp baking powder
2 tsp cinnamon
4 oz /100g caster sugar
4 oz /100g soft brown sugar
4 oz/100g melted butter
6 oz/175g grated parsnip
4 oz/100g grated cooking apple
3 eggs
1 tbsp milk

Topping

8 oz/225g cream cheese
2 oz/50g butter
8 oz/225g icing sugar
1 tsp lemon juice

Method

1. Sieve the flour, baking powder and cinnamon together.
2. Mix all dry ingredients together.
3. Add the melted butter to the parsnips and apples along with the eggs and milk.
4. Mix all ingredients together and pour into greased lined 9 inch cake tin and bake for approximately 35 - 40 minutes.
5. Meanwhile make the topping.
6. Drain all the liquid off the cream cheese.
7. Mix the cream cheese and butter together.
8. Sieve the icing sugar and add along with the lemon juice to the mixture.
9. Spread on top of the cake and decorate as desired.

This is an unusual cake but very tasty

Mandarin Tea Cup Cakes

4 oz/100g softened butter
4 oz/100g caster sugar
2 eggs
4 tsp jam (of your choice)
10 fl oz/300ml double cream for decoration

1 312g tin of mandarin oranges
7 oz/175g self-raising flour
4 x 6-7oz tea cups

Method

1. Cream the softened butter and sugar together.
2. Gradually add in the eggs and 1 dsp of mandarin juice.
3. Sieve the flour and gently fold in.
4. Gently stir in 2 tbsp of mandarins leaving some for decoration.
5. Grease all 4 tea cups.
6. Place a spoonful of jam at the bottom of each one.
7. Divide the mixture between the cups, filling each one three parts full.
8. Stand the cups in a roasting tin filling half way up the cup with water.
9. Place in the oven for approximately 30 - 35 minutes until they are soft but firm to touch on top.
10. Leave to cool.
11. Whip the cream up and pipe on top of each one. Decorate with remaining mandarins.

These tea cup cakes look and taste nice for a special occasion.

Margaret's Celebration Fruit Cake

4 lb/1.8kg mixed dried fruit	1lb 8oz/700g self-raising flour
½ pint/300ml brandy	6 oz/175g cherries
1 lb/450g soft brown sugar	8 oz/225g ground almonds
1 tbsp treacle	2 tsp mixed spice
1 lb/450g butter	1tsp nutmeg
8 medium eggs	Grated rind of 1 lemon

Method

1. Soak the mixed dried fruit in the brandy overnight.
2. Line a 10" Square cake tin first with brown paper then double line with greaseproof paper.
3. Cream the butter, sugar and treacle together.
4. Whisk the eggs together in a separate bowl.
5. Gradually add in the eggs along with 3 tbsp of flour.
6. Slowly add in the fruit and mix.
7. Lastly add in all the dry ingredients along with the cherries and mix until well combined.
8. Pour the mixture into the prepared cake tin and cover with greaseproof paper.
9. Bake at 150°C 300°F gas 3 for 1 hour then turn down to 140°C 275°F gas 1 for a further 3 hours.

I use this recipe for all my celebration cakes and has always proven to be very popular.

Pink Paradise Cake

10 oz/275g caster sugar
10 oz/275g self-raising flour
1 tsp baking powder
6 fl oz/175ml vegetable oil
2 eggs
1tsp red food colouring
1tsp vanilla extract
7 fl oz/200ml milk

Filling

1 lb/450g icing sugar
8 oz/225g cream cheese
4 oz/100g butter

Method

1. Mix together sugar, oil and eggs.
2. Sieve the flour and baking powder.
3. Add the vanilla extract and red colouring to the milk and stir.
4. Add the milk mixture alternately with the sieved flour into the egg mixture and mix well together.
5. Bake in a greased lined 10 inch cake tin for approximately 30-35 minutes.
6. Meanwhile make the filling: mix together the cream cheese, butter and icing sugar together.
7. When the cake has cooled, cut in half and spread with the cream cheese mixture saving some to spread over the top of the cake.

A lovely moist cake ideal for a party.

Robert's Chocolate Log

3 eggs
4 oz/100g caster sugar
 3 oz/75g self-raising flour
½ oz/20g cocoa powder

Filling and Icing

6 oz /175g butter
8 oz/225g icing sugar
1 oz/25g cocoa powder

Method

1. Whisk the eggs and sugar until a thick creamy mixture.
2. Sieve the flour and cocoa powder together and fold into the egg mixture with a metal spoon.
3. Pour the mixture into a greased lined 9"x12" Swiss roll tray.
4. Bake for 15 minutes.
5. Make the butter cream by creaming all the ingredients together.
6. When baked, turn the sponge onto a sugared sheet of greaseproof paper and roll up.
7. When cooled unroll and spread with the chocolate butter cream saving some for the outside.
8. Roll up again carefully and spread the outside with the remaining butter cream.
9. Decorate with holly and sieved icing if desired. Alternatively you can fill with freshly whipped cream.

Scrumptious Lemon Madeira Loaf

4 oz/100g margarine
5 oz/150g caster sugar
6 oz/175g self-raising flour
¼ tsp baking powder
2 eggs
Zest and juice of 1 lemon

Method

1. Cream margarine and sugar together.
2. Sieve the flour and baking powder together.
3. Beat the eggs and lemon juice together adding to the mixture alternately with the sieved flour and baking powder.
4. Lastly stir in the zest and juice of the lemon.
5. Line and grease a 2lb loaf tin.
6. Pour mixture into loaf tin and bake for 40 minutes until firm to touch.

A very moreish and refreshing loaf. Ideal for an afternoon tea.

Sponge Parkin

4 oz/100g margarine
8 oz/225g self-raising flour
4 oz/125g granulated sugar
2 tsp ground ginger
¼ tsp bicarbonate of soda
1 egg
5 fl oz/150ml boiling water
1 tbsp black treacle

Method

1. Rub margarine into dry ingredients.
2. Add in the egg and mix.
3. Mix the boiling water and the treacle together and add to the mixture mix until well combined.
4. Pour the mixture into a greased lined 2lb loaf tin.
5. Bake for approximately 40 minutes until firm to touch.

This loaf is quite a wet mixture so gives a nice moist texture. It's best kept in an airtight container for a couple of days prior to serving.

Sticky Loaf

8 oz/225g self-raising flour
5 oz/150g soft brown sugar
4 oz/100g margarine
2 eggs
2 tbsp marmalade
2 tbsp apple juice or cider
6 oz/175g mixed dried fruit
2 oz/50g cherries

Method

1. Sieve the flour.
2. Place flour, sugar, margarine and eggs into mixing bowl and mix until a smooth dough.
3. Add marmalade and apple juice and mix again.
4. Mix in fruit and cherries.
5. Place mixture into a lined greased 2lb loaf tin.
6. Bake for 40 minutes.

A lovely moist loaf best kept for a couple of days before eating.

Suzanne's Chocolate Mayo Cake

10 oz/275g self-raising flour
¼ tsp baking powder
2 oz/50g cocoa powder
3 oz/75g chocolate drops
6 oz/175g brown sugar
6 oz/175g mayonnaise
9 fl oz /300ml boiling water
1tsp vanilla essence

Topping

2 oz/50g dark chocolate
4 oz/100g butter soft
8 oz/225g icing sugar
1tsp vanilla extract

Method

1. Grease and line an 8 inch round cake tin.
2. Sieve the flour, baking powder and cocoa powder together.
3. Place all the dry ingredients into mixing bowl and mix well.
4. Add mayonnaise, boiling water and vanilla essence and mix thoroughly.
5. Pour mixture into prepared tin.
6. Bake at 170°C 325°F gas 3 for approximately 40-45 minutes until firm to touch.
7. Leave to cool before turning out.
8. Make the topping.
9. Melt the chocolate in a bowl over a pan of hot water.
10. Beat the soft butter, icing sugar and vanilla together.
11. Fold in the melted chocolate until completely mixed adding a little milk if it's too stiff.
12. When the cake has completely cooled spread the topping over the top.

Alternatively you can use a chocolate butter cream filling and topping, see page 155.

Serve cold or warmed up with ice cream.

A very moist moreish cake; my children's favourite.

Whisked Sponge Mix

3 oz/75g self-raising flour
1 oz/25g cornflour
1 tsp baking powder

4 egg yolks
6 oz/175g caster sugar

Filling

3 tbsp raspberry jam

10 fl oz/150ml double cream

Method

1. Sieve together the flour, baking powder and cornflour.
2. Separate the eggs.
3. Whisk the egg whites until they stand in peaks. Gradually add in the sugar.
4. Whisk the egg yolks and add to the egg whites. Whisk altogether.
5. Fold in the flour with a metal spoon.
6. Divide the mixture equally between two 9 inch round greased and lined tins.
7. Bake for approximately 30 - 35mins until springy to touch.
8. Meanwhile whip the cream until thick.
9. When the cake has cooled sandwich together with the raspberry jam and double cream.

A beautiful light refreshing cake.

Cookies & Buns

Cherry Cookies

Oven 170°C / 325°F / Gas 3

4 oz /100g margarine
6 oz /175g caster sugar
10 oz /275g self-raising flour
1tsp vanilla extract
1 egg
4 oz /100g cherries
1 tbsp milk

Method

1. Crumb together margarine sugar and flour until resembles breadcrumbs.
2. Stir in 3oz/75g cherries (leaving some for the tops).
3. Add the vanilla milk and egg and mix together until it forms a firm dough (do not over mix).
4. Roll out into 12 balls golf ball size.
5. Place onto a lightly floured baking tray and flatten each one slightly.
6. Place half a cherry in the centre of each one.
7. Place in the oven and bake 170°C 325°F gas 3 for approximately 25 - 30 minutes.

These cookies are great snacks for when the children come home from school.

Chocolate Chip Muffins

Oven 170°C / 325°F / Gas 3

5 oz/150g caster sugar
3 fl oz/75ml olive oil
1 egg
7 fl oz/200ml milk

2 oz/50g cocoa powder
6 oz/175g self-raising flour
½ tsp baking powder
2 oz/50g dark or white chocolate chips

Method

1. Beat together sugar, oil and egg.
2. Sieve together flour, cocoa and baking powder.
3. Add the milk alternately with the flour into the egg mixture.
4. Fold in the chocolate chips.
5. Divide the mixture between 9 muffin cases.
6. Bake for approximately 25 minutes.
7. Decorate if desired with butter cream page 154.

These chocolate muffins are loved by everyone.

Chocolate Cookies

Oven 170°C / 325°F / Gas 3

4 oz/100g margarine
4 oz/100g caster sugar
4 oz/100g brown sugar
8 oz/225g self-raising flour
1 oz/25g cocoa powder
5 oz/150g chocolate drops
2 eggs
2 tsp vanilla extract

Method

1. Mix all dry ingredients together along with the margarine.
2. Beat together eggs and vanilla and add to the dry ingredients.
3. Mix until a firm dough. (Do not over mix).
4. Roll into 15 - 18 golf ball sized rounds and flatten slightly.
5. Place on a lightly floured baking tray.
6. Bake at 170ºC 325°F gas 3 for 20 minutes.
7. Leave to cool before packing.

Good party treats.

Gingerbread Shapes

8 oz/225g plain flour
1 tsp baking powder
2 tsp ground ginger

4 oz/100g butter
3 oz/75g brown sugar
1 tbsp syrup
1 tbsp treacle

Method

1. Sieve the flour, ginger and baking powder together.
2. Place the butter, sugar, syrup and treacle into a saucepan to melt.
3. Pour the melted mixture into the flour and mix.
4. Knead together into a ball.
5. Dust a surface with flour and roll out till about ½ cm thick.
6. Cut out into shapes and place onto a baking tray leaving space in between each one.
7. Bake for 15 - 20 minutes.
8. Leave to cool before you move them.
9. Decorate if desired with melted chocolate or water icing, see page 163.

A nice treat for the children.

Ginger Nut Biscuits

3 oz/75g caster sugar
9 oz/250g self-raising flour
1tsp baking powder
1 tsp ginger
4 oz/100g butter
3 oz/75g syrup
1 egg

Method

1. Mix all dry ingredients together.
2. Melt the butter and syrup in saucepan.
3. Add all the dry ingredients along with the egg and mix.
4. Roll the dough into small balls and place onto a greased baking tray.
5. Bake at170°C 325°F gas 3 for 15 - 20 minutes.
6. Leave to cool and store in an airtight container.

Madeleines

4 oz/100g butter
4 oz/100g caster sugar
2 eggs
1 tsp vanilla extract
4 oz/100g self-raising Flour

1 jar raspberry jam
8 oz/225g desiccated coconut
4 oz/100g glace cherries

Method

1. Cream the butter and sugar together.
2. Beat the eggs and vanilla extract and add to the creamed mixture.
3. Sieve the flour and fold into the creamed mixture.
4. Grease 6 dariole moulds and fill each one three parts full with the mixture.
5. Bake for approximately 25 minutes.
6. When baked trim off the bottoms so they sit upright.
7. Melt the jam in a saucepan.
8. Brush each madeleine with a pastry brush till each one is covered in jam.
9. Now roll each one in the desiccated coconut and decorate with a cherry on top.

Madeleines always look and taste good especially for afternoon tea.

Melting Moments

6 oz/175g margarine
4 oz/100g caster sugar
1 egg
1 cap vanilla essence
10 oz/275g self-raising flour
Coconut to coat
A cherry for decoration

Method

1. Cream the margarine and sugar together.
2. Beat in the egg and vanilla essence followed by the flour. Do not over-mix at this stage.
3. Mould into about 16 rounds golf ball size.
4. Roll each one in coconut and place on a baking tray.
5. Flatten slightly then place ½ cherry in each one.
6. Bake at 170°C 325°F gas 3 for 20 minutes.
7. Store in an airtight container.

Melt in the mouth ideal for children.

Raspberry & Lemon Muffins

8 oz/225g self-raising flour
½ tsp baking powder
4 oz/100g caster sugar
1 lemon grated rind
2 eggs
4 fl oz/100ml soured cream
4 tbsp olive oil
6 oz/175g raspberries

Method

1. Sieve the flour and baking powder together.
2. Add the sugar and lemon rind to the sieved mixture.
3. Beat the cream egg and oil together.
4. Add the oil mix into the dry ingredients and mix until combined.
5. Fold in the raspberries with a metal spoon.
6. Divide the mixture between 12 muffin cases.
7. Bake at 170ºC 325ºF gas 3 for 25 minutes.

Beautiful light and refreshing summer muffins.

Raspberry Cushions

6 oz/175g margarine
10 oz/275g self-raising flour
4 oz/100g caster sugar
1 egg
A little milk
Raspberry jam for filling

Method

1. Rub fat into dry ingredients.
2. Add egg and a little milk mix until firm. Do not over mix at this stage.
3. Roll into 10 -12 golf ball sizes.
4. Place onto a lightly floured baking tray.
5. Dip the back of a spoon into flour and make a hole in the centre of each one, then place a spoonful of jam in each one.
6. Bake at 170°C 325°F gas 3 for 20 - 25 minutes.
7. Leave to cool before serving.

Rocky Buns

1 lb/450g self-raising flour
4 oz/100g brown sugar
4 oz/100g caster sugar
4 oz/100g sultanas
4 oz/100g raisins
8 oz/225g margarine
2 eggs
2 tbsp milk

Method

1. Crumb all dry ingredients along with margarine.
2. Add in the milk and eggs a little at a time.
3. Mix until a stiff dough.
4. Mould into 12 Rocky Buns and place on a greased baking tray.
5. Bake at 170°C 325°F gas 3 for 30 - 35 minutes.
6. Store in an airtight container.

Alternatively you can use cherries or chocolate drops instead of fruit.

Simple Cookies

Oven 170°C / 325°F / Gas 3

12 oz/350g self-raising flour
8 oz/225g butter
4 oz/100g caster sugar
1 orange grated rind

Method

1. Place the flour, butter and orange rind into a bowl and mix until like breadcrumbs.
2. Add the sugar and mix until a firm dough.
3. Roll out about ½ inch or 1 cm thick.
4. Lightly flour a baking tray and cut out cookies or different shapes.
5. Bake for 15 - 20 minutes.
6. Leave to cool then dust with icing sugar.

These cookies are what it says: simple but tasty.

Sugar & Spice Cookies

12 oz/350g plain flour
1 tsp baking powder
1 tsp nutmeg
½ tsp cinnamon
¼ pt/150 ml milk

4 oz/100g butter
8 oz/225g caster sugar
1 tsp vanilla extract
1 egg
Demerara sugar for decoration

Method

1. Sieve the flour, baking powder and spices together.
2. Cream together butter, sugar and vanilla until light.
3. Add the egg to the creamed mixture.
4. Add the sieved flour alternately with the milk until a soft dough. Do not overmix at this stage.
5. Place in a polythene bag and chill for 30 minutes.
6. Roll out onto a floured surface, cutting with a round cutter about ½ inch thick.
7. Transfer onto a lightly floured baking tray and sprinkle with the demerara sugar.
8. Bake for 12 - 15 minutes until golden.

Sweet Pastry Mince Pies

Pastry

12 oz/350g plain flour
6 oz/175g margarine
2 oz/50g caster sugar
2 fl oz/55ml milk

Filling

1 large 440g jar of mincemeat
2 dsp brandy

Method

1. Crumb margarine and flour.
2. Mix sugar and milk together. Add the sugar solution to the flour mix.
3. Mix until all combined and your mixing bowl is clean. Refrigerate for 30 minutes.
4. Meanwhile make the filling by mixing the brandy in the mincemeat.
5. Flour 2 x 12 pate tins.
6. Roll out half the pastry thinly and cut out 24 bases.
7. Lightly dust the pate tins with flour; this helps them to not stick.
8. Line the pate tins with the bases and place in 1 heaped teaspoon of mincemeat.
9. Roll out the other half and using a star cutter, cut out 24 lids for the pies.
10. Place lids firmly on top and bake for approximately 25 - 30 minutes.
11. Leave for 5 minutes and then take out of tins carefully lifting them with a knife and place onto a cooling rack.

A very popular mince pie recipe one which I always use as they melt in your mouth.

Treacle Delights

4 oz/100g butter
4 oz/100g caster sugar
2 tbsp treacle
4 oz/100g self-raising flour
2 oz/50g coconut
4 oz/100g rolled oats
A little milk if required

Method

1. Place butter, sugar and treacle in a saucepan and bring to the boil.
2. Meanwhile mix all dry ingredients together.
3. Pour the boiled mixture over dry ingredients stir and leave to stand for 30 minutes.
4. At this stage you can add a little milk to make a softer consistency if desired.
5. Roll into balls by dipping your hands in cold water first; this will stop the mixture from sticking to your hands. This mix will make about 20 Treacle Delights.
6. Bake for 15 - 20 minutes.
7. Leave to cool and set as they will be soft when you take them out of the oven.

Treacle Delights are good all year round but especially good for children at Halloween.

Viennese Fingers

Oven 170°C / 325°F / Gas 3

10 oz/275g butter
8 oz/225g caster sugar
12 oz/350g self-raising flour
1 tsp vanilla extract

Method

1. Cream butter and sugar together until soft and creamy.
2. Add the flour and vanilla beat well until piping consistency.
3. Grease a baking tray.
4. Using a piping bag pipe, pipe about 12 fingers.
5. Bake at 170°C 325°F gas 3 for approximately 15 minutes.
6. When baked leave to cool and sandwich together with butter cream, see page 159.

Tray Bakes

Autumn Tray Bake

8 oz/225g butter
8 oz/225g caster sugar
8 oz/225g self-raising flour
½ tsp baking powder
1 tbsp cinnamon
1 tbsp nutmeg
3 eggs
5 fl oz creme fraise

Method

1. Cream the butter and sugar together.
2. Sieve the flour, baking powder and spices together.
3. Gradually add in the eggs alternately with the flour.
4. Add in the creme fraise and mix.
5. Pour the mixture into a lined 11x 8 inch tray.
6. Bake at 170ºC 325ºF gas 3 for approximately 35 minutes.
7. Store in an airtight container.

A lovely light and refreshing tray bake with a hint of spice.

Chocolate Berry Squares

4 oz/100g butter
2 oz/50g cocoa powder
8 oz/225g brown sugar
6 oz/175g self-raising flour
2 eggs
4 oz/100g frozen berries

Toppings

3 oz/75g caster sugar
2 oz/50g self-raising flour
2 oz/50g soft butter
1 egg
3 oz/75g grated plain chocolate

Method

1. Place the butter, cocoa and sugar into a saucepan and stir until melted. Remove from the heat.
2. Sift the flour and stir into the melted mixture along with the eggs.
3. Stir in the frozen berries.
4. Pour the mixture into a greased lined 11 x 8 inch baking tray.
5. Make the topping.
6. Beat all ingredients together except the chocolate until smooth.
7. Spread over the base.
8. Bake for about 45 minutes until firm to touch.
9. Sprinkle with grated chocolate.
10. Cool and cut into squares.

A very moreish tray bake with lots of flavour.

Above: Autumn Tray Bake
Below: Chocolate/Orange & Caramel Shortbread

Above: Coconut & Fruit Slices
Below: Chocolate Berry Squares

Chocolate/Orange & Caramel Shortbread

Shortbread

12 oz/350g plain flour
9 oz/250g butter
4 oz/100g caster sugar
2 oz/50g rice flour
Zest of 1 orange

Caramel

4 oz/100g butter
2 oz/50g caster sugar
2 tbsp syrup
397g 1 small tin of condensed milk

Topping
8 oz/225g plain chocolate melted

Method

1. Make the shortbread first by placing all the ingredients in a mixing bowl and mixing until a firm dough.
2. Grease and line a 9 x 12 inch baking tray.
3. Roll shortbread into the tray and bake at 170°C 325°F gas 3 for 30 minutes.
4. Meanwhile make the caramel by placing all ingredients in saucepan and stirring on a gentle heat, bring to the boil and simmer for 8 minutes.
5. Remove from the heat and beat well.
6. When shortbread is baked pour over the caramel and leave to set in the fridge.
7. When set pour over the melted chocolate. Leave to set again and cut into fingers.

A delicious shortbread with an orange flavour coming through.

Cornflake Squares

8 oz/225g butter
6 oz/175g caster sugar
1tbsp syrup
8 oz/225g cornflakes
4 oz/100g porridge oats

Method

1. Place butter, sugar and syrup in a pan and melt.
2. Crush cornflakes with your hands.
3. Add cornflakes and oats to the melted mixture.
4. Place mixture into an 11 x 8 inch lightly greased baking tray and spread evenly.
5. Bake for 15 - 20 minutes.
6. Mark into squares whilst still warm. Pack when cold.

A tray bake that children just love.

Cream Cheese Squares

5 oz/150g butter
6 oz/175g soft brown sugar
2 eggs
10 oz/275g self-raising flour
6 oz/175g cream cheese
4 oz/100g plain chocolate chips

Method

1. Cream the butter and sugar together.
2. Beat in the eggs.
3. Gradually add in the flour and mix until creamy.
4. Beat the cream cheese and chocolate chips together and stir into the mixture.
5. Spread mixture into a greased lined 9 x 9 inch deep baking tray.
6. Bake at 170°C 325°F gas 3 for 30 - 35 minutes.

Date and Orange Squares

8 oz /225g dates
¼ pt water
4 oz/100g sugar
Juice of 1 orange
7 oz/200g margarine
12 oz/350g porridge oats

Method

1. Place dates, orange juice and water in a pan along with the sugar and simmer until soft.
2. Melt margarine in a pan.
3. Add porridge oats to the date mixture followed by the melted margarine.
4. Mix thoroughly together.
5. Place mixture into a greased 9 x 9 inch baking tray.
6. Bake at 170°C 325°F gas 3 for 25 minutes.
7. Mark into squares while still warm.
8. Leave to cool before packing.

Flapjacks

6 oz/175g butter
4 oz/100g brown sugar
2 tbsp golden syrup
1 lb/450g porridge oats

Method

1. Place butter, sugar and syrup in a saucepan on a medium heat until melted.
2. Remove from heat and stir in porridge oats.
3. Place mixture in a greased 9 x 9 inch tray and press firmly down.
4. Bake at 170°C 325°F gas 3 for 30 minutes until golden brown.
5. Leave to cool for 5 minutes then mark into fingers.
6. Pack when cold.

Left: *Flapjack*

Below: *Suzanne's Chocolate Strawberry Crumble Slices (Page 98)*

Fudge Brownies

4 oz/100g dark chocolate
6 oz/175g butter
6 oz/175g caster sugar

4 eggs
8 oz/225g self-raising flour
4 oz/100g toffee fudge caramels
2 fl oz/55ml milk or cream

Method

1. Melt the chocolate and butter in a pan or microwave.
2. Remove from the heat and stir in the sugar.
3. Beat the eggs lightly and stir into the melted chocolate.
4. Fold in the flour.
5. Melt the toffee along with the milk or cream.
6. Whilst the toffee is melting line a 10 x 8 inch baking tray.
7. When the toffee has melted, gently fold in to the chocolate mix and transfer into the prepared baking tray.
8. Bake for 30 - 35 minutes.
9. Leave to cool before packing.

A delicious and very moreish brownie.

Lime and Coconut Fingers

Oven 170°C / 325°F / Gas 3

8 oz/225g digestive biscuits
4 oz/100g butter
Small 397g can condensed milk
6 oz/175g desiccated coconut
Grated rind of a lime

Topping

8 oz/225g icing sugar
Juice of 1 lime
2 tbsp water

Method

1. Crush biscuits in a bag with a rolling pin.
2. Place butter in a saucepan along with the milk.
3. Add biscuits, coconut and lime rind to the melted mixture. Mix altogether.
4. Spread mixture into a 9 x 9 inch baking tray.
5. Bake for 20 minutes.
6. Make the icing: mix the icing sugar, lime juice and water together.
7. When the tray bake has cooled, spread lime icing over the top and leave to set before serving.

This tray bake is very light and refreshing

Top Left: Marshmallow Maltesers Tiffin

Above: Assorted Cookies

Left: Lime and Coconut Fingers

Marshmallow Malteser Tiffins

8 oz/225g dark chocolate
4 oz/100g butter
2 tbsp syrup
4 oz/100g digestive biscuits   Topping
4 oz/100g Maltesers   8 oz/225g dark chocolate
4 oz/100g coloured marshmallows   1 oz/25g butter

Method

1. Melt the chocolate, butter and syrup in a basin over a pan of boiling water.
2. Crush the biscuits and Maltesers in a plastic bag leaving a few chunky bits.
3. Stir the biscuits, Maltesers and marshmallows into the melted mixture.
4. Line an 11 x 8 inch deep tray.
5. Press mixture into prepared tray and place in fridge for 15 minutes.

Topping

6. Melt the chocolate and butter in a basin over a pan of boiling water. When melted pour over tray bake.
7. Refrigerate for 2 hours before cutting.

A very colourful and scrummy tiffin which doesn't last very long when children are around.

Peppermint Slices

4 oz/100g margarine
4 oz/100g caster sugar
8 oz/225g self-raising flour

Topping

12 oz/350g icing sugar
4 tbsp warm water
1 tsp peppermint essence
2 tsp green colouring
8 oz/225g plain chocolate

Method

1. Cream the margarine and sugar together. Stir in the flour until combined.
2. Press the mixture into a 9 x 12 inch shallow lined baking tray.
3. Prick with a fork and bake at 170°C 325°F gas 3 for 15 minutes until golden.
4. Make the topping: mix the icing sugar with the warm water, peppermint and green colouring together.
5. When the base has cooled, spread peppermint mix over the base and leave to set.
6. When set, melt the chocolate in a bowl over a pan of hot water and pour over the peppermint.
7. Leave to set and cut into slices.

Coconut & Fruit Slices

8 oz/225g sweet pastry (see recipe page152)
3 tbsp strawberry jam
4 oz/100g margarine
4 oz/100g caster sugar
4 eggs

8 oz/225g dried fruit (sultanas, raisins)
4 oz/100g coconut
2 oz/50g broken walnuts
4 oz/100g broken cherries
2 oz/50g self-raising flour

Method

1. Line a 9 x 9 inch deep tray with sweet pastry.
2. Spread the jam over the pastry.
3. Cream margarine and sugar together.
4. Add coconut, fruit and walnuts and mix well.
5. Now add the eggs followed by the cherries and flour. Mix altogether.
6. Spread over the pastry base and bake for 30 - 35 minutes until firm.
7. Leave to set.
8. Cut into fingers.

This tray bake is very popular with all the different flavours coming through.

Roger's Chocolate Biscuit Tray Bake

4 oz/100g butter
4 oz /100g plain chocolate
1 small 397g can condensed milk
4 oz/100g raisins
12 oz/350g digestive biscuits
2 oz/50g chopped white chocolate buttons
6 oz/175g melted chocolate for the topping

Method

1. Melt butter and chocolate in a heatproof bowl. Place the bowl into a pan of hot water and heat until the chocolate and butter have melted. (The reason for doing it this way is to prevent the chocolate from burning).
2. Remove from heat and add in condensed milk and raisins.
3. Crush biscuits roughly with a rolling pin in a plastic bag.
4. Add biscuits and chopped white chocolate buttons to the melted ingredients and stir well.
5. Turn mixture into an 11 x 8 inch greased lined baking tray.
6. Pour the topping over and leave to set in the fridge.
7. Cut and serve as desired.
8. Best served from the fridge.

A very scrummy no bake biscuit tray bake with lots of different textures.

Shortbread

12 oz/350g plain flour
9 oz/250g butter
4 oz/100g caster sugar
2 oz/50g ground rice

Method

1. Place all ingredients in a bowl and mix until well combined.
2. Roll out into a 9 x 12 inch greased lined baking tray.
3. Bake 170°C 325°F gas 3 for 20 - 35 minutes until golden brown.
4. Mark into fingers whilst still warm and sprinkle with caster sugar.
5. Leave to cool before packing.

To make Cherry Shortbread add 2oz/50g cherries into the mixture.

Walnut Fingers

8 oz/225g brown sugar
6 oz/175g butter
2 eggs
1tsp vanilla extract
9 oz/250g self-raising flour
6 oz/175g broken walnuts

Topping

6 oz /175g dark chocolate

Method

1. Cream the butter, sugar, eggs and vanilla together until soft.
2. Sieve the flour and fold in along with the walnuts.
3. Line and grease a 9 x 9 inch deep baking tray.
4. Press mixture firmly into tray.
5. Bake at 170°C 325°F gas 3 for 25 - 30 minutes until firm.
6. Remove from oven and grate chocolate on top whilst still hot.
7. Mark into portions then leave to set before packing.

Suzanne's Chocolate Strawberry Crumble Slices *Oven 170°C / 325°F / Gas 3*

10 oz/275g self-raising flour
4 oz/100g caster sugar
8 oz/225g butter
8 oz/225g porridge oats
3 tbsp strawberry jam
4 oz/100g plain chocolate drops
1 oz/25g flaked almonds

Method

1. Rub together flour, butter and sugar until like breadcrumbs.
2. Stir in the porridge oats.
3. Press ¾ of ingredients firmly into a greased lined 11 x 8 baking tray and bake for 15 minutes until golden.
4. Leave to cool then spread with strawberry jam and sprinkle with chocolate drops.
5. Spread remaining crumble mix on top, pressing down firmly followed by the flaked almonds on top and return to the oven for a further 20 minutes until golden brown.
6. Leave to cool and mark into fingers.

A very moist and moreish tray bake.

Scones

Apple Scones

Oven 170°C / 325°F / Gas 3

1 lb/450g self-raising flour
½ tsp baking powder
4 oz/100g butter
4 oz/100g caster sugar
1 cooking apple
2 oz/50g sultanas
7 fl oz/200ml milk

Method

1. Sieve the flour and baking powder together.
2. Crumb the flour, butter and sugar together.
3. Peel, core and chop the apple into small pieces.
4. Add the apple and sultanas to the mixture and mix.
5. Gradually add in the milk and mix until the mix forms a soft dough.
6. Roll out onto a floured surface and cut out with a plain or fluted cutter.
7. Place onto a baking tray and bake for approximately 15 - 20 minutes until golden brown.
8. Leave to cool.

Serve with butter and a nice cup of tea.

Cheddar & Walnut Scones

Oven 170°C / 325°F / Gas 3

2 oz/50g crushed walnuts
4 oz/100g self-raising flour
4 oz/100g wholemeal flour
2 oz/50g butter
3 oz/75g grated cheddar cheese
3 fl oz/75ml milk

Method

1. Sieve the flours together.
2. Place all ingredients together except for the milk.
3. Mix until like breadcrumbs.
4. Gradually add in the milk until rolling consistency.
5. Roll out on floured surface and cut 8 medium scones.
6. Place on a lightly floured baking tray and bake for approximately 20 minutes until golden brown.

These scones are best served warm with butter and a little extra cheese.

Frozen Berry Scones

1 lb/450g self-raising flour
½ tsp baking powder
4 oz/100g butter
4 oz/100g caster sugar
4 oz/100g frozen berries (For example, blackcurrants, raspberries, redcurrants)
7 fl oz/200ml milk

Method

1. Sieve together flour and baking powder.
2. Add the butter and sugar and rub in until like breadcrumbs.
3. Add in ½ the milk followed by the frozen berries.
4. Add in remaining milk, do not over mix at this stage otherwise your mix will become very sticky.
5. Roll scone mixture out onto a floured surface and cut around 10 - 12 scones about ½ inch thick.
6. Transfer onto a lightly floured baking tray.
7. Brush tops with milk and Bake at 170°C 325°F gas 3 for approximately 20 - 25 minutes.
8. Cool on a wire cooling rack.

Delicious served with jam and freshly whipped cream or just butter.

Fruit Scones

1 lb/450g self-raising flour
½ tsp baking powder
4 oz/100g butter
4 oz/100g caster sugar
6 oz /175g mixed fruit (sultanas and raisins)
7 fl oz/200ml soured cream or milk

Method

1. Sieve together flour and baking powder.
2. Rub fat into dry ingredients.
3. Gradually add in liquid and mix until a firm soft dough.
4. Roll out on to a floured surface and cut out with a plain or fluted cutter. The mixture makes about 10 - 12 medium size scones.
5. Place on a lightly floured baking tray and bake at 170°C 325°F gas 3 for approximately 20 minutes until golden brown.

Ready to be served with lashings of jam and cream.

Cherry Scones

1lb /450g self-raising flour
½ tsp baking powder
4oz /100g butter
4oz/100g caster sugar
6oz/175g Cherries
7 fl oz/200ml soured cream or milk

Method

1. Rub butter into dry ingredients.
2. Gradually add in liquid and mix until a firm dough.
3. Roll out on a floured surface and cut out with a plain or fluted cutter the mixture makes about 10-12 medium size scones.
4. Place on a lightly floured baking tray and bake at 170°C 325°F gas 3 for approximately 20 minutes until golden brown.

An easy way to see if your scones are baked is to tap the bottom and if they sound as if they are hollow they are baked.

Ready to serve with lashings of cream.

Lavender Scones

1 lb/450g self-raising flour
½ tsp baking powder
4 oz/100g butter
4 oz/100g caster sugar
2 tsp dried lavender buds
1 egg
5 fl oz/150ml soured cream or milk

Method

1. Sieve the flour and baking powder together.
2. Place all dry ingredients into mixing bowl along with the butter.
3. Mix until like breadcrumbs.
4. Beat the egg and milk together and gradually add to the crumbed mixture.
5. Mix until a soft dough and the bowl is clean.
6. Roll out onto a floured surface and cut out about 12 – 14 scones with a plain or fluted cutter.
7. Place scones on a lightly floured baking tray and bake at 170°C 325°F gas 3 for about 20 minutes.
8. Leave to go cool and serve with lashings of butter and cream.

A special treat for Mother on Mothering Sunday

Lemonade Scones

12 oz/350g self-raising
¼ pt 150ml double cream
¼ pt/150ml lemonade
Grated rind of 1 lemon

Filling

8 oz/225g lemon curd
10 fl oz/275ml double cream

Method

1. Mix the flour and lemon rind together.
2. Add the cream and lemonade gradually until the mixture forms a soft dough.
3. Roll out onto a floured surface and cut out with a plain or fluted cutter.
4. Place on a lightly floured baking tray and bake for approximately 15 - 20 minutes until golden brown.
5. Leave to cool.
6. Whip the cream until thick. Slice the scones and fill with lemon curd and cream.

A very light refreshing scone with a taste of a difference.

Pies and Desserts

Apple & Blackcurrant Pie

1 lb/450g sweet pastry (page 152)
6 oz/175g washed blackcurrants
5 large cooking apples
4 fl oz/120ml water
4 oz/100g granulated sugar

Method

1. Roll ½ the pastry into a pie dish and blind bake for 15 minutes.
2. Peel, core and slice the apples. Place into a saucepan along with the sugar and water. Cook until soft.
3. Stir in the blackcurrants and cook for a further 5 minutes.
4. Cool slightly then pour into pastry case.
5. Roll out remaining pastry to make the lid.
6. Dampen the pastry edge with water or beaten egg and cover with the lid.
7. Trim seal and flute the edge.
8. Use pastry trimmings to decorate pie as desired.
9. Make small hole in the top for any steam to escape.
10. Brush with beaten egg or milk to glaze.
11. Place on a baking tray and return to the oven for 30 - 35 minutes.

This pie can be served either hot or cold with custard or cream ….very moreish either way.

Top Left: Egg Custard
Top Right: Apple Lattice
Left: Apple and Blackcurrant Pie.

Apple Lattice Pie

12 oz/350g mix of sweet pastry (page 152).
1 lb/450g cooking apples
¼ pt/150ml water
4 oz/100g granulated sugar
½ tsp nutmeg
4 oz/100g raisins or sultanas

Method

1. Line a pie dish with sweet pastry saving 4oz/125g for the lattice top.
2. Bake blind for 15 - 20 minutes. (see pastry page 149)
3. Peel, slice and core the apples and place into a saucepan along with the sugar, water, nutmeg and raisins. Simmer for 10 minutes until they become soft.
4. When the pastry base is cooked pour in the apple mix.
5. Roll out the pastry into strips and lay diagonally across the pie dampen the edges with water so they will stick to the pie edge.
6. Return to the oven for a further 20 minutes.

A lovely lattice pie having the nutmeg flavour coming through. Serve with either custard or cream.

Banana Flan

8 oz/225g sweet pastry (page 152).
½ pt /300ml milk
4 egg yolks
4 oz/100g caster sugar
2 bananas
1 oz/25g cornflour

Method

1. Line an 8 inch flan ring with the sweet pastry and bake blind (see pastry page 149).
2. Whisk the egg yolks and sugar in a bowl until almost white.
3. Mix in the cornflour.
4. Boil the milk in a thick bottomed pan.
5. Whisk the milk onto the egg yolks, sugar and cornflour and mix well.
6. Return to the pan and bring to the boil.
7. Slice one banana and mix into the filling.
8. Pour mixture into baked flan case and sprinkle with caster sugar to prevent skin from forming.
9. Leave to set and decorate with sliced banana.

Baked Cheesecake

Biscuit base

3 oz/75g melted butter
6 oz/175g plain chocolate digestive biscuits

Cheese filling

1 lb/450g full fat cream cheese
4 oz/100g creme fraise
3 oz/75g caster sugar
1 lemon juice and rind
5 egg yolks
1tsp vanilla extract
2 tbsp gelatine

Method

1. Crush the biscuits by placing into a bag and crushing with a rolling pin.
2. Add the melted butter to the biscuits and mix well together.
3. Line an 8" flan dish with the biscuit base pressing down with the back of a metal spoon.
4. Make the cheesecake filling by creaming the cheese, crème fraise, caster sugar, lemon rind and juice together.
5. Add the egg yolks and vanilla. Whisk until a firm mixture.
6. Dissolve the gelatine in a small amount of boiling water and add to the mixture.
7. Pour the mixture into the biscuit base and bake in a slow oven for 45 - 50 minutes until set.

This cheesecake can be served as it is or it can be decorated with fresh fruit. Very light and refreshing.

Banoffi Pie

Base

9 oz/250g ginger nut biscuits
4 oz/100g butter

Topping

4 - 5 bananas
10 fl oz/300ml double cream
1tsp instant coffee

Filling

1 large 397g can condensed milk

1 oz/25g icing sugar
Grated plain chocolate

Method

1. Crush the ginger nuts in a plastic bag with a rolling pin.
2. Melt the butter on the stove and add in the crushed ginger nuts.
3. Spoon the biscuit mix into a greased lined flan dish pressing down with the back of a metal spoon.
4. Immerse the unopened can of condensed milk into a pan of boiling water cover and simmer for 3 hours. This will turn into toffee.
5. Meanwhile whip the cream, coffee and icing sugar until thick.
6. Empty the can of toffee into the flan base and spread evenly.
7. Slice the bananas over the top of the toffee.
8. Spread the cream over the top followed by the grated chocolate.

Basic Meringues

2 egg whites
4 oz/100g caster sugar

Filling

10 fl oz/300ml double cream

Method

1. Place egg whites into a sterilized mixing bowl and whisk until they form soft peaks.
2. Add in ½ the sugar and whisk again.
3. Repeat with remaining sugar.
4. Either pipe or spoon the mixture onto a baking tray lined with parchment paper. This mixture will make 6 - 8 meringues depending on the size you pipe them.
5. Bake in a slow oven 140°C 275°F gas 1 for approximately 2 hours until they are dry and quite crisp.
6. Meanwhile whip the cream for the filling.
7. Fill the meringues with cream and decorate as desired.

For a contrast you can dip the bases of meringues in melted chocolate before filling with cream.

Berry Fruit Cobbler

6 oz/175g self-raising flour
2 oz/50g butter
2 oz/50g caster sugar
Milk to combine
1 lb/450g fresh berries (For example, raspberries, blackberries, redcurrant..)

Method

1. Rub the flour with the butter and sugar until like bread crumbs.
2. Add the milk and mix until a rolling out consistency.
3. Leave to rest for a while in the fridge.
4. Place the berries in a pan with the water and cook until soft.
5. When cooked pour into a pie dish.
6. Roll out the cobbler topping out onto a floured surface and cut out 8 cobblers about 2½ cm. thick.
7. Place the cobblers on top of the berries and cook for 35 minutes.
8. Serve with custard.

A quick and refreshing dessert.

Choux Buns

¼ pint/150ml water
2 oz/50g butter
2½ oz/60g plain flour sieved
2 eggs

Topping

4 oz/100g melted chocolate

Filling

½ pint/300ml double cream

Method

1. Put the water and butter into a saucepan and bring to the boil.
2. Remove from the heat and beat in the flour to form a ball and it leaves the sides of the pan clean.
3. Leave the mixture to cool slightly. Beat in the eggs one at a time.
4. Spoon the mixture into a piping bag with a star or plain nozzle.
5. Pipe golf ball size balls onto a greased baking tray.
6. Bake 180°C 350°F gas 4 for 25 - 30 minutes until the bottoms sound hollow when you tap them.
7. Leave to cool and cover each one with melted chocolate.
8. Whip the cream up. Make a small hole in each one at the base and pipe cream into the hole.

Always a popular dessert.

Classic Summer Pudding

6 - 8 slices of bread with crusts removed
2 lb/900g fresh or frozen mixed fruit (For example, raspberries, gooseberries, blackberries, strawberries)
¼ pt/150ml water
6 oz/175g caster sugar

Method

1. Line a 2 pint/1.2 litre pudding basin with bread cutting each piece in half and arranging it to fit around the basin overlapping it slightly leaving a couple of pieces for the top.
2. Place all the fruit into a saucepan along with the water and sugar. Heat gently until all the fruit is soft and the juices begin to run.
3. Using a large sieve, place the fruit into the bread lined basin leaving some to one side for decoration.
4. Place the remaining two pieces of bread on top of the fruit folding in the pieces around the outside of the basin.
5. Press down firmly and place a saucer or small plate on top.
6. Leave in the fridge for 4 - 5 hours whilst the juices soak through into the bread.
7. Turn out onto a plate and decorate with remaining fruit.

Serve with fresh cream.

Damson Flapjack Crumble

1lb/450g damsons
4 oz/100g granulated sugar
10 fl oz/300 ml water

Flapjack

6 oz/175g butter
4 oz/100g brown sugar
2 tbsp golden syrup
12 oz/350g porridge oats

Method

1. Place damsons into a saucepan along with the sugar and water.
2. Leave on a low heat until the damsons are soft.
3. Meanwhile make the flapjack: melt the butter, sugar and syrup in a saucepan over a gently heat.
4. Remove from the heat and stir in the oats.
5. Remove the damsons from the heat and pour into a pie dish (its optional if you want to remove the stone at this stage).
6. Spread the flapjack mixture over the damsons and bake at 170°C 325°F gas 3 for 20 - 25 minutes.

Serve with lashings of custard or ice cream.

Top: Mum's Lemon
        Meringue Pie
Left: Damson Flapjack
        Crumble

Egg Custard Tart

8 oz/225g sweet pastry (recipe page 152)
10 fl oz/300ml single cream
3 eggs
2 oz/50g caster sugar
1tsp vanilla essence
Ground nutmeg for sprinkling on top

Method

1. Line a pie dish with sweet pastry and prick holes in the bottom.
2. Bake blind for 15 minutes (see pastry page).
3. Meanwhile make the custard mix.
4. Whisk eggs, vanilla and sugar together.
5. Add the cream to the egg mixture whisk altogether.
6. Pour custard mix into baked flan dish and sprinkle nutmeg on top.
7. Return to the oven and bake for a further 25 minutes until set.

Fresh Fruit Crumble

1 lb/450g fresh fruit of your own choice
4 oz/100g granulated sugar
½ pint/300 ml water

Crumble

6 oz/175g plain flour
4 oz/100g gran sugar
2 oz/50g porridge oats (optional)
2 oz/50g butter

Method

1. Place fruit, sugar and water in a saucepan and leave to simmer for 10 - 15 minutes.
2. Make the crumble: crumb all the ingredients together until like breadcrumbs.
3. Remove fruit from stove and pour into pie dish.
4. Spread crumbed mixture over the top and bake at 170°C 325°F gas 3 for 30 minutes.

Serve hot or cold with either custard or cream.

Mandarin Rice Dessert

1 oz/25g butter
1 pint/570ml milk
4 oz/100g pudding rice
1 oz/25g caster sugar
2 eggs yolks separated
1 312g can mandarin oranges
1 tsp vanilla extract

Topping

2 egg whites
2 oz/50g caster sugar

Method

1. Melt the butter in a pan. Add the rice and milk bring to the boil and simmer until thick and creamy.
2. Drain the mandarin oranges then arrange in a greased deep flan dish leaving a few for decoration.
3. Once the rice mixture is reasonably thick, take off the heat and add in the egg yolks, sugar and vanilla.
4. Pour over the mandarin oranges in the flan dish. Place in the fridge for 20 minutes until set.
5. Meanwhile make the topping: whisk the egg whites till stiff. Add the caster sugar and whisk again.
6. Once the rice mixture has set, add on the meringue and decorate with mandarins.
7. Place under grill until golden brown.

Frozen Loaf Dessert

½ pint/300ml double cream
3 tbsp sherry
6 meringue shells crushed

1 tbsp icing sugar
4 oz/100g frozen fruit

Topping

6 oz/175g frozen fruit
2 oz/50g granulated sugar
2 tbsp water

Method

1. Whisk the cream until thick. Add in the sherry and whisk again.
2. Fold in the crushed meringue followed by the frozen fruit and icing sugar.
3. Line a loaf tin with greaseproof paper. Spoon the mixture into the loaf tin and flatten with a palette knife.
4. Place a piece of greaseproof on the top and place into the freezer for 2 - 3 hours.
5. Meanwhile make the topping: place all the ingredients into a saucepan and cook until a soft puree.
6. Remove from the heat and set aside until cold.
7. When you remove the loaf from the freezer tip out onto a plate. If it is difficult to remove place the bottom of the tin in boiling water for 2 seconds and tip out.
8. Pour the topping over the loaf and serve immediately.

This dessert is lovely and will keep for 3-4 months in the freezer.

Hot Chocolate Pudding

2 oz/50g butter
3 oz/75g caster sugar
2 eggs separated
12 fl oz/350ml milk
2 oz/50g self-raising flour
2 dsp cocoa powder heaped

Method

1. Cream the butter and sugar together until pale.
2. Beat in the egg yolks.
3. Stir in the milk.
4. Sift the flour and cocoa powder together.
5. Add the flour to the creamed mixture and mix well.
6. Whisk the egg whites until stiff and fold into the mixture.
7. Pour mixture into a greased ovenproof dish.
8. Bake at 170°C 325°F gas 3 until spongy to touch.

This pudding is magic the way it separates: sponge at the bottom, mousse in the centre and a layer of sponge on top. Served with either cream or lashings of custard.

Kiwi & Strawberry Pavlova

6 egg whites
12 oz/350g caster sugar
Pinch of salt

Filling

10 fl oz/275ml double cream
3 kiwi fruit
1 punnet strawberries

Method

1. Put the egg whites in a large clean sterilized mixing bowl. Whisk until they start to form peaks.
2. Gradually add in the sugar whisking after each addition until it forms soft glossy peaks.
3. Spoon or pipe the mixture onto 2 parchment lined baking trays, each about an 8 inch/20cm diameter.
4. Bake in a slow oven 140°C 275°F gas 1 for approximately 2 hours or until the outside is crispy.
5. Meanwhile whip the cream until thick and wash, peel and slice the kiwi and strawberries.
6. When the meringues have cooled, sandwich together with the cream and some of the kiwi and strawberries saving some for decoration on the top.

The meringue can be made up to 10 days before you want to use it as long as it's stored in an airtight tin.

Lemon Tart

Pastry

8 oz/225g sweet pastry
4 oz/100g butter
3 oz/75g caster sugar
2 egg yolks
8 oz/225g plain flour

Filling

5 eggs
4 oz/100g caster sugar
5 fl oz/150ml double cream
Juice and zest of 2 lemons
1 lemon sliced for decoration
Oven 150°c 300°f gas 2

Method

1. Make the pastry as page 152.
2. Line an 8 inch/20 cm flan dish with pastry. You can freeze any leftover pastry.
3. Blind bake (see pastry page 149) at 170°C 325°F gas 3 for 15 minutes.
4. Take out rice paper and bake for a further 10 minutes.
5. Make the filling by whisking all ingredients together and pouring into tart base.
6. Place in a slow oven 150°C 300°F gas 2 until set.
7. Leave to cool and decorate with sliced lemon.
8. Serve with pouring cream.

A very refreshing lemon tart with rich pastry.

Mum's Lemon Meringue Pie

Oven 170°C / 325°F / Gas 3

8 oz/225g sweet pastry, see page 152
½ pint/ 300ml water
2 lemons grated rind and juice
2 oz/50g cornflour

3 eggs separated
1 oz/25g butter
4 oz/100g sugar

Method

1. Line a pie dish with the sweet pastry and blind bake (see pastry page 152) for 20 minutes.
2. Put the grated rind and juice along with the cornflour into a bowl along with 2 tbsp of water and mix till a smooth paste.
3. Bring the remaining water to the boil and pour over the cornflour mix.
4. Return to the stove and bring to the boil simmer for 3 minutes until thick.
5. Remove from the heat and add in the egg yolks and sugar.
6. Pour the mixture into the prepared flan case.
7. Now make the meringue topping by whisking the egg whites until they form peaks then adding the sugar a little at a time whisking well after each addition.
8. Spoon the meringue on top of the lemon filling and either bake until golden brown or place under the grill until golden brown.

When baking blind place a piece of greaseproof paper in the base followed by chickpeas or rice.
This lemon pie was always a family favourite served every Sunday lunch.

Old Fashioned Eves Pudding

Oven 170°C / 325°F / Gas 3

1 lb/450g cooking apples
4 oz/100g caster sugar
2 fl oz/50ml water
4 oz/100g butter
2 eggs
4 oz/100g self-raising flour sieved

Method

1. Peel, core and slice the apples.
2. Arrange the apples at the bottom of a pie dish.
3. Scatter 2oz/50g of sugar over the apples and pour over the water.
4. Cream the butter and remaining sugar together.
5. Beat in the eggs followed by the flour.
6. Spread the mixture over the apples.
7. Bake in a moderate oven 170°C 325°F gas 3 for 35 - 40 minutes until firm to touch.

Serve with lashings of custard.

Peach Pudding

1 x 410g can of peaches,
3 oz/75g butter
3 eggs separated
2 oz/50g self-raising flour
Milk made up to 1 pint with the drained peach juice.
2 oz/50g caster sugar

Topping

3 egg whites
2 oz/50g caster sugar

Method

1. Drain, peaches and cut up into cubes. Retain the juice.
2. Melt the butter in a saucepan.
3. Take off heat and sprinkle in the flour and mix.
4. Add milk and juice mixture and gradually bring to the boil. Simmer for 2 minutes.
5. Take off heat and add egg yolks and sugar.
6. Pour mixture over peaches and place in slow oven to set 150°C 300°F gas 3 for 35 - 40 minutes.
7. Meanwhile, make the topping: whisk the egg whites and sugar together until stiff.
8. Spoon the mixture on top of the peach pudding peaking it with the back of a spoon.
9. Place under a grill until golden.

Queen Victoria's Pudding

4 eggs separated
1 pint/600ml milk
4 oz/100g breadcrumbs
5 tbsp raspberry jam
4 oz/100g caster sugar

Method

1. Beat the egg yolks.
2. Stir in the milk, then the breadcrumbs.
3. Spread the jam at the bottom of a pie dish.
4. Pour the milk mixture over the jam and leave to stand for ½ hour.
5. Bake at 150°C 300°F gas 2 for about 45 minutes until set.
6. Meanwhile whisk the egg whites until stiff and fold in the sugar.
7. Pile the meringue on top of the pudding and return to the oven for a further 15 minutes until golden brown.

A good old traditional pudding.

Rich Chocolate Torte

8 oz/225g sweet pastry, see page 152
8 oz//225g dark chocolate
½ pint/300ml double cream
1 tbsp crème fraise

Topping

¼ pint/150ml double cream
4 oz/100g grated chocolate

Method

1. Roll out the pastry into a pie dish and blind bake (see pastry page 152) for 15 - 20 minutes.
2. Melt the chocolate in a basin over a pan of hot water.
3. Place the cream and crème fraise into a saucepan and bring to the boil.
4. When chocolate has melted, pour over the boiled cream and mix well.
5. Pour mixture into prepared pastry and leave to set.
6. Make the topping: whip the cream until thick and pipe on top as desired.
7. Sprinkle grated chocolate on top.

A very rich chocolate dessert but one you can't refuse.

Steamed Syrup Pudding

6 oz/175g butter
6 oz/175g caster sugar
3 eggs
7 oz /200g self-raising flour
1 dsp milk
3 tbsp golden syrup

Method

1. Cream butter and sugar together.
2. Beat the eggs and add alternately with the flour.
3. Add in the milk and mix.
4. Pour the syrup into a well-greased 1½ pint pudding basin followed by the sponge mixture.
5. Place in a steaming pan with greaseproof paper tied loosely around the top steam for approximately 1½ hours until firm on top.
6. When steamed, turn out onto a large plate so the syrup runs down the sides. Serve immediately.

Syrup pudding is delicious served with custard.

Teacake Butter Pudding

4 large tea cakes
4 oz/100g dried fruit
4 oz/100g caster sugar
4 eggs
10 fl oz/300ml single cream
10 fl oz/300ml milk
2 tsp cinnamon

Method

1. Slice the teacakes in 3 and butter them then cut in half.
2. Arrange the teacakes in a greased pie dish.
3. Cover tea cakes with the dried fruit.
4. Whisk the sugar, eggs, cream and milk together.
5. Pour egg mixture over the teacakes.
6. Sprinkle on the cinnamon.
7. Bake 170°C 325°F gas 3 for approximately 40 minutes.

A delicious teacake pudding with spices coming through.

Syllabub

1 lemon grated rind and juice
¼ pint/150ml sweet sherry
1 tbsp white wine
3 oz/75g caster sugar
½ pint/275ml double cream

Method

1. Mix together lemon, rind, sugar, sherry and wine until dissolved.
2. Add cream and whisk till the mixture thickens and forms soft peaks.
3. Pour into individual glasses and leave for a few hours.
4. Decorate with either grated nutmeg or a slice of lemon.

A very refreshing dessert.

If you want it to go a little further, add two stiffly whisked egg whites after you have whisked the cream in and you will gain a couple more syllabubs.

Pastry Making

Top Tips for Perfect Pastry

1. Always use a good quality plain flour for pastry making.

2. Self-raising flour can be used, but more often than not use plain flour for pastry for lining pie dishes and topping pies. Self-raising can be used when making a suet pastry as you need that extra lift.

3. Always use a good quality fat as this will determine the flavour as well as the texture of the pastry. Traditional recipes use half lard and half butter which still can be used but I prefer to use all butter or a good quality margarine.

4. Whist making pastry use ice cold water a little at a time to bind your flour and fat together as too much water will produce a hard crust on a finished pie and too little will make pastry difficult to roll.

5. If you want to add flavour to your pastry add a little lemon juice.

6. Adding egg yolk to pastry makes it richer and gives a good colour.

7. Roll one side of pastry only and always in the same direction.
    Turn the pastry rather than the rolling pin.
    Never stretch pastry as it will shrink once baked.

8. Utensils need to be kept as cool as possible.
    Roll out on a cold surface.
    Keep hands cool.

Blind Baking

Baking blind is the process of baking a pastry base without the filling. Line a pie dish as required with pastry followed by greaseproof paper placing uncooked rice chick peas or baking beans in and bake for 15 - 20 minutes. This will prevent the base from going soggy when making certain pies – for example, egg custard.

Rich Sweet Pastry

6 oz/175g plain flour
4 oz/100g butter
2 oz/50g icing sugar
1 egg yolk
2 tbsp cold water

Method

1. Sieve the flour into a large bowl.
2. Cut the butter into cubes and rub into the flour.
3. Sieve the icing sugar into the mixture.
4. Beat the egg and add to the mixture along with the water. Add a little extra water if needed.
5. Mix until a dough.
6. Wrap in polythene and leave to rest in a cool place for half an hour before use.

Ideal for special occasion, fruit flans and tarts.

Shortcrust Pastry

6 oz/175g plain flour
Pinch of salt
3 oz/75g butter
2 tbsp cold water

Method

1. Sieve the flour and salt together.
2. Cut the butter into cubes and using your fingertips rub into the flour until the mixture resembles breadcrumbs.
3. Gradually add in the cold water and mix until it forms a dough and the sides of the bowl are clean. If needed add a little more water.
4. Wrap pastry into polythene and leave to rest in a cool place until required.

This pastry can be used either for sweet or savoury pies but omit the salt if using for sweet pies.

Sweet Pastry

12 oz/350g plain flour
6 oz/175g margarine
2 oz/50g caster sugar
2 fl oz/ 55ml milk

Method

1. Crumb margarine and flour.
2. Mix sugar and milk together.
3. Add sugar solution to the flour mix.
4. Mix until all combined and your mixing bowl is clean.
5. Refrigerate for 30 minutes before use.
6. Roll out as desired.

This pastry has proven to be extremely popular and is very versatile. It can be used for all sweet pies. It also freezes very well if you don't require it all at one time.

Top tier: Meringues
Middle tier: Mince pies
Bottom tier: Chocolate chip and
Raspberry/Lemon Muffins

Useful Recipes

Butter Cream

6 oz/175g butter
8 oz/225g icing sugar
2 dsp milk

Method

1. Sieve the icing sugar and mix all ingredients together until a creamy white consistency.
2. Use as required.

Butter cream will keep for a few days if kept covered in a fridge.

For chocolate flavour add 2 dsp cocoa powder.
For coffee flavour add 1 dsp instant coffee dissolved in 1 dsp of hot water.
For lemon flavour use the zest of 1 lemon and 2tsp lemon juice
For orange flavour use zest of 1 orange and 2 tsp orange juice.
For vanilla flavour add 2 tsp vanilla extract.

Cream Cheese Frosting

2 x 280g packs of cream cheese
4 oz/100g butter
1 lb/450g icing sugar
1 tsp vanilla essence

Method

Mix all ingredients together until a soft consistency.

Cream cheese frosting is a nice topping for muffins. It also can be used for fillings and toppings for carrot cakes and sponges and makes a nice change from butter cream.

Damson Gin

1 lb/450g washed damsons
1 lb/450g granulated sugar
750 ml gin

Method

1. Prick damsons with a fork.
2. Sterilize 4 bottles with lids by either soaking in hot water for 10 minutes or putting them through the dishwasher on a hot wash if you have one.
3. Leave to air dry.
4. Alternately add damsons, sugar and gin to each jar.
5. Give each jar a good shake and place in a dark place. (This will help to keep the colour).
6. Leave for 3 months giving it a good shake from time to time.
7. Strain with a piece of muslin and decant into bottles.

If you want a less syrupy gin put a little less gin in.

Ideal for Christmas time. Just be patient and leave for 3 months to get the best results.

Damson Jam

3 lb/1.4kg damsons
1 pint/570ml water
3 lb/1.4kg sugar
Wax paper disks
Makes 1½ - 2lb (750-1kg) jam

Method

1. Wash and take stalks off damsons.
2. Pour the water and damsons into a thick bottomed large saucepan.
3. Bring the damsons to the boil and simmer until damsons are soft. At this stage you can take the stones out if you wish.
4. Add the sugar and stir bring to the boil.
5. Test with a sugar thermometer reading 105°C 220°F setting point. Alternatively, use the cold saucer test: put 1 tsp of jam onto a cold saucer allow to cool for 1 minute. Push the surface of the jam with your finger tip; if the surface wrinkles setting point has been reached.
6. Leave to stand for 5 minutes.
7. Pour jam into jam pots. Whilst still warm place a wax disk on top and seal with a lid.
8. Label jars with date and flavour of jam.
9. Best left for a couple of months before eating.

Margaret's Mulled Wine

1 bottle of red wine
½ bottle white wine
1 litre carton tropical juice
1 litre carton apple juice
1 tsp nutmeg
3 cinnamon sticks
8 oz/225g demerara sugar
1 orange stuck with cloves
1 apple sliced
1 orange sliced

Method

1. Place all ingredients into a large pan.
2. Stir until sugar has dissolved.
3. Leave on a low heat for 1 hour but do not boil.
4. Test for sweetness; if you like it sweet you may need a little more sugar.
5. Leave to stand before serving.

Best made the day before. This recipe was always very popular at Christmas at Tatton when we were serving 400 people every evening for 7 days. Bear in mind I have reduced the recipe quantities above.

Strawberry Jam

6 lb/3kg strawberries
Juice of 2 lemons
6 lb/3kg sugar

Makes 10lb/4.5kg

Method

1. Wash the strawberries and place in a thick bottomed pan with the lemon juice.
2. Place on the stove and simmer until reduced by one third.
3. Remove from the heat and add in the sugar.
4. Stir, return to the heat and bring to the boil until setting point test with a sugar thermometer 105°C 220°F. If you don't have one you can do the cold saucer test by placing a tsp of jam onto a cold saucer leaving a minute then push the surface with your finger tip if the surface wrinkles the jam is ready.
5. Sterilize 4 jam jars by either soaking in hot water for 10 minutes with the lids or putting them through a dishwasher on a hot wash if you have one.
6. Whilst the jars are still warm pour the jam into them placing a wax disk on top of each one.(this prevents a skin from forming) leave to cool before putting the lids on.
7. Label with date and name of jam.
8. Best left for a couple of months before eating.

Treacle Toffee

8 oz/225g black treacle
1 lb/450g brown sugar
8 oz/225g butter
1 tsp water
½ tsp lemon juice

Method

1. Place the treacle, sugar, butter and water into a saucepan. Heat gently.
2. Stir until all ingredients are completely dissolved.
3. When the mixture has dissolved add the lemon juice continuously stirring and boiling until the mixture hardens when dropped in cold water or if you have a sugar thermometer boil until 140°C 275°F.
4. Pour mixture into a well-greased baking tray and leave to harden.
5. Once hardened turn out onto a wooden board and break into pieces.

To test in cold water fill a cup half full with cold water and with a spoon just drop a spoonful of the treacle mix into the water. If it's ready it will form a ball.

Vanilla Ice Cream

3 eggs separated
2 oz/50g icing sugar
1 vanilla pod
10 fl oz/300ml double cream

Method

1. Whisk the egg yolks, vanilla pod and icing sugar until pale and creamy.
2. Whisk the cream until thick.
3. In another bowl whisk the egg whites until firm.
4. Fold the cream carefully into the egg yolk mixture.
5. Lastly fold the egg whites into the egg mixture.
6. Pour the ice cream into a lined loaf tin and freeze for 2 hours.
7. Serve as desired.

Very refreshing in the summer months.

Water Icing

4 oz/100g icing sugar
1 tbsp/15ml water

Method

1. Sieve the icing sugar.
2. Pour the water into the icing sugar and mix.
3. Colour the icing at this stage if desired.
4. Spread the icing over the cake and leave to set.

Trouble Shooting in Cake Making

Your cake is very dense	Too much liquid or sugar. Baked in too cool of an oven.
Holes in the cake	Not mixed properly.
Dry cakes	Too much flour or cocoa powder. Over baked cake.
A crumbly cake that sticks to the tin	Cake tin not lined properly.
A cake that rises then sinks	Oven not calibrated properly. Possibly too much baking powder.
Cake is sticky in centre	Cake not cooked long enough.
Cake cracked and peaked in centre	Too much baking powder. Oven too hot.

Index

Notes

Notes